ALL ABOUT
My Precious Baby

Positively Pregnant!

The day I found out you were on your way to me...

_____

_____

_____

_____

_____

Your First Photoshoot

All about your first ultrasound...

_____

_____

_____

_____

_____

All About Mommy

Full Name _____ Birthdate _____

Where I was born _____

Some of my favorite hobbies _____

_____

_____

_____

_____

Some of my favorite childhood memories _____

_____

_____

_____

_____

What I wanted to be when I grew up _____

MY FAVORITE...

Color _____ Food _____

Holiday _____ Music _____

Pictures of Mommy

All About Daddy

Full Name _____ Birthdate _____

Where I was born _____

Some of my favorite hobbies _____

_____

_____

_____

_____

Some of my favorite childhood memories _____

_____

_____

_____

_____

What I wanted to be when I grew up _____

MY FAVORITE...

Color _____ Food _____

Holiday _____ Music _____

Pictures of Daddy

Mommy as a baby

Daddy as a baby

How you look like mom

How you look like dad

_____

_____

_____

_____

_____

_____

_____

_____

_____

_____

_____

_____

_____

_____

You as a baby

Your Family Tree

Mother

_____

Father

_____

Grandfather

_____

Grandmother

_____

Grandfather

_____

Grandmother

_____

Great Grandfather

_____

Great Grandmother

_____

Great Grandmother

_____

Great Grandfather

_____

Great Grandfather

_____

Great Grandmother

_____

Great Grandmother

_____

Great Grandfather

_____

Foods I LOVED to eat & craved....

_____

_____

_____

_____

All About Mommy's Pregnancy

Song's & shows I watched and
listened to all the time...

_____

_____

_____

_____

Foods & smells I COULDN'T STAND...

_____

_____

_____

_____

When I first felt you move:

_____

_____

When your dad first felt a kick:

_____

_____

How we felt when we found out...
boy or girl:

_____

_____

_____

_____

_____

Who threw it for us: _____

Where: _____

When: _____

Foods we had: _____

Games we played: _____

Gifts:

_____   _____

_____   _____

_____   _____

_____   _____

_____   _____

_____   _____

Your Babyshower

Pictures!

The Day You Arrived

When I started labor: _____

When you were born: _____

Where you were born: _____

Who was at your birth: _____

_____

Story of your birth from Mom: _____

_____

_____

_____

_____

_____

_____

Visitors after you were born: _____

_____

Birthing complications? _____

_____

Story of your birth from Dad:

_____

_____

_____

_____

_____

_____

_____

Proud Mama

Proud Daddy

Perfect Baby

Full name: _____

Time of Birth: _____

Weight: _____   Height: _____

Hair Color: _____

The Day You Were Born

Day of the week: _____

The weather: _____

#1 Song: _____

#1 Movie: _____

#1 Book: _____

Famous People who share your birthday: _____

_____

Zodiac: _____

Birthstone: _____

World Population: _____

Most popular baby names this year: _____

_____

Historical Events: _____

_____

Your Name...

Names we considered for you:

_____

_____

_____

_____

_____

Why we chose your name:

_____

_____

_____

_____

_____

The best parts of having you home:

_____

_____

_____

_____

You At Home

The craziest parts of having you home:

_____

_____

_____

_____

1 Week Old

Weight: _____ Height: _____

Thing's you're loving: _____

New things you're doing this week: _____

_____

A few of your firsts this week:

_____

_____

_____

_____

_____

Favorite moments with you this week:

2 Weeks Old

Weight: _____ Height: _____

Favorite things to do with you: _____

New adventures with you this week: _____

_____

Letter From Mom

3 Weeks Old

Weight: _____ Height: _____

Things you're starting to do this week: _____

_____

_____

Letter From Dad

_____

_____

_____

_____

_____

_____

_____

_____

_____

_____

1 Month Old

Weight: _____ Height: _____

You're favorite things to do nowadays: _____

_____

_____

New things your trying and loving:

_____

_____

_____

_____

_____

Your newest adventures are:

2 Months Old

Weight: _____ Height: _____

New things you started this month: _____

_____

_____

3 Months Old

Weight: _____ Height: _____

New things you started this month: _____

_____

_____

4 Months Old

Weight: _____ Height: _____

New things you started this month: _____

_____

_____

5 Months Old

Weight: _____ Height: _____

New things you started this month: _____

_____

_____

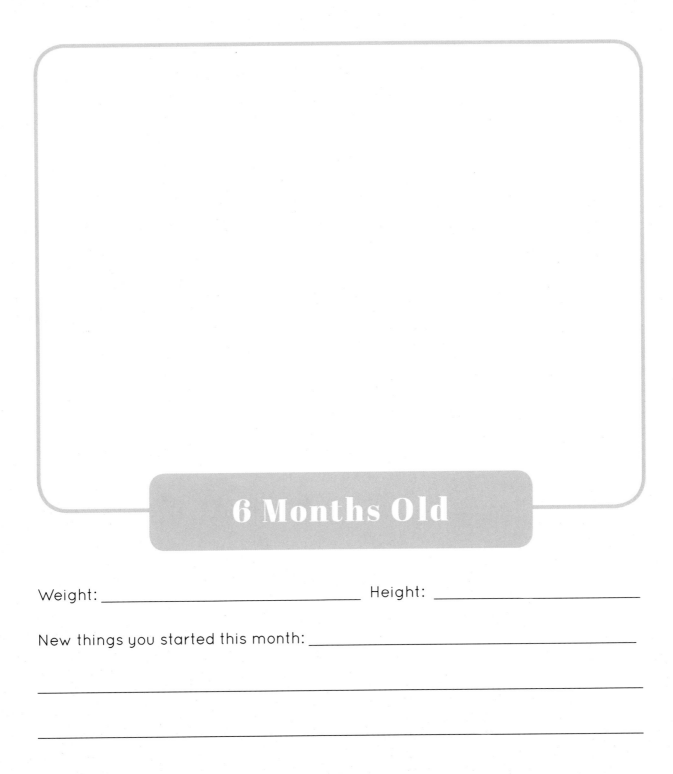

6 Months Old

Weight: _____ Height: _____

New things you started this month: _____

_____

_____

8 Months Old

Weight: _____ Height: _____

New things you started this month: _____

_____

_____

10 Months Old

Weight: _____ Height: _____

New things you started this month: _____

_____

_____

1 Year Old

Weight: _____ Height: _____

Your favorite foods and snacks: _____

_____

_____

Your Firsts...

Started holding your head up:

_____

Started reaching for things:

_____

Started smiling:

_____

Rolled over the first time:

_____

Started scooting around:

_____

Started eating solid foods:

_____

Started standing up to things:

_____

Started crawling:

_____

Started dancing to music:

_____

First time laughing:

_____

First word:

_____

First steps:

_____

Your first solid food was:

_____

First favorite song:

_____

Everyone we invited to celebrate:

_____

_____

_____

_____

_____

Your First Birthday Party!

Foods, games and music:

_____

_____

_____

_____

Gifts you got:

_____

_____

_____

_____

pssst...
that's you!

BEAUTIFUL DESIGNS FOR BEAUTIFUL PEOPLE

www.loveablefringe.com

Made in the USA
Monee, IL
13 May 2022

96361117R00026